"A Story of

The Journey of a Lost Boy of Sudan

Written by

Deng Ajak Jongkuch and Lisa Frankel Wade

Illustrated by Tereese Smaldino Radenbaugh

ISBN: 145656885X
ISBN 13: 9781456568856
LCCN: 2011901308

A Story of Hope—The Journey of a Lost Boy of Sudan

By Deng Ajak Jongkuch and Lisa Frankel Wade

This is a story that might never have happened. If Deng Jongkuch, the boy in this story, had stopped even once and lost his hope, we would not know about him at all. But instead, we know his story because he never lost hope, and his hope gave him courage, and his courage brought him to a place where he could give others courage and strength. This is his story. It is about a boy who is no longer lost, but is now a man who has found his voice, and a mission.

Deng—His Early Years

Deng Ajak Jongkuch was born in 1981[1] in the rural village of Gwalla in Southern Sudan. Deng and most of the people of his village are part of the Dinka tribe, the largest tribe in Southern Sudan. His name, in the language of the Dinka tribe, means "rain."

Deng's country, Sudan, is the largest country on the continent of Africa. It is divided into two regions—Northern and Southern Sudan[2]. Sudan is about one-fourth the size of the United States and is approximately seven

---

1. Actually, Deng's true birth date is unknown. When the boys in the refugee camps were documented, many of them did not know their birth dates, so they were given the birth date of January 1 and a year that approximated their age. Deng says he might have been born in the middle of 1981, but he is not sure.

2. In January of 2011 the people of Southern Sudan voted to become a separate nation from the rest of Sudan. There will now be two separate countries - Northern Sudan and Southern Sudan. Southern Sudan will become a separate nation on July 9, 2011.

thousand miles away from New York City. Over forty million people live in the country, and there are over five hundred different tribes. The most common religious practice in Northern Sudan is Muslim, while the religion in Southern Sudan is mostly Animist and Christian. The government of Sudan has its headquarters in the North, where there are good schools and hospitals and an educated population. Southern Sudan is the part of the country that has good soil and water for agriculture, and the people who live there are mostly farmers and cattle herders who are not highly educated. The rich soil is a great resource for the country, since this is where food is grown. Southern Sudan also has oil reserves, and Northern Sudan wants access to them.

In his early years, Deng lived with his mother and father in his village. Villagers enjoyed milk and meat from the goats and cattle they herded, and ate vegetables and fruit that grew on their land. The women of the village made grain from grinding the corn that they grew. There was no electricity or running water, so the women went to the village well every day to get clean water. Families lived in simple huts made of mud and straw. Deng enjoyed playing in the fields with other children. Life was peaceful and uncomplicated in the village.

Fighting Begins

But outside the village, the country of Sudan was in conflict. There were great differences in the lives of the people in Northern and Southern Sudan. The people who lived in Northern Sudan and the villagers of Southern Sudan were fighting over religion, land, and resources.

Because the people lived in different regions and spoke different languages, it was difficult for them to sit down and communicate with one another. Because they could not understand each other easily, it was more challenging to work through their disagreements peaceably. The result of this lack of communication was that the villagers were often subjected to violence, being attacked with guns by government soldiers sent from the North. To defend their villages, Southern Sudan formed a rebel militia.

The attacks between the government soldiers from Northern Sudan and the rebel militia in Southern Sudan became more frequent, and a terrible civil war started. In a civil war the people are not fighting against another country—they are fighting against each other—their own countrymen.

Deng Must Escape from His Village

One night in 1987, when Deng was only five years old, his village was attacked by soldiers from Northern Sudan. There was so much noise—guns, yelling, animals screeching and howling, and the roar of fire as the village was being set ablaze. There was terror, confusion, fire, and smoke. The government soldiers kidnapped many of the young girls for slaves and teen boys for the army, and many adults were killed. Younger boys who were close to Deng's age had a chance to escape by running away.

Fearing for his life, Deng ran away
from his hut into the surrounding
jungle to take cover in the trees.

10

With no clothes on his back or shoes on his feet, he ran for his life in the middle of the night. He was soon far from his village, frightened, sad, and confused, and separated from his mother and father. In the morning, Deng discovered that about fifty other young boys also ran from his village. He only saw two adults. Deng was happy to find four young boys who were his cousins, but he did not see his mother or father. Deng and his four cousins decided to stay together. It was lucky that one of the boys had grabbed an old blanket and another an empty plastic jug before they escaped into the jungle.

The group of five boys didn't know what to do, so they began walking very fast following a dirt path in the jungle with the other boys who had escaped. The two adults in the small group told the boys that they heard it was safe in the neighboring country of Ethiopia, because that was the base for the militia of Southern Sudan. The adults directed the group in the direction of Ethiopia.

Deng was scared and confused, but he knew he must stay with his cousins and walk with the others from his village. Deng's urge to survive was very strong, and he was helped by a special gift his mother and father had given him. This was the gift of hope in his heart. Deng remembered his parents' words to him: "Never give up hope, Deng, no matter what happens." As he kept walking farther away from the danger of his village and the terrible cruelty of the soldiers there, he began to see hope in everything—in the rocks along his path, in the birds singing in the trees above, in the frogs croaking in the ponds beside the road. "Don't give up hope!" they all seemed to say, as he trudged on his journey to find safety. His hope kept him walking among jungle trees and through large grassy plains called savannahs. His hope kept him walking forward even through his fears.

Deng Begins His Long Journey with Other Lost Boys

Soon, Deng and the boys from his village were joined by other young boys, who were escaping from their villages, too. There were only a few adults in the group, who helped lead and provide direction to Ethiopia. The boys had no shoes and no clothes. As the boys walked, they saw lions, gazelles, crocodiles, antelopes, and zebras.

Food was scarce in the jungle. The boys ate wild fruit and vegetables and small rodents. Sometimes they worked together as a group to chase and kill a large animal such as a gazelle. They roasted the animals they killed over a fire that they started by rubbing two branches until they made a spark, which lit the kindling made of dried grass and branches.

Sometimes the group went for two days without water. The small amount of water they had was stored in plastic gallon containers, which they would fill when they found water. They would share sips of it, rationing just enough for everybody each day. If one boy took three sips, they all took three sips, and no more. They were very careful about cooperating, because they knew that was the way to survive. Deng and his cousins felt very lucky to have a plastic container to store and share water.

13

It was hot in the jungle so the group walked early in the morning when it was cooler. They slept in the afternoon when it was hottest and then started walking again at dusk until about midnight. The boys did not have mats to sleep on, but Deng and his cousins were happy to sleep under the tattered blanket they shared.

Although they were very tired, hungry, and scared, by staying together as a group they were able to support and help each other to feel a sense of safety, even when it was dark and scary.

Sometimes Deng didn't think he could walk any farther—his feet hurt so badly, and his stomach was growling from hunger and thirst. But he remembered his parents' words to him, and he kept walking. He still hoped to find a safe village; he hoped he would find a place to rest and a place where he could find food. But most of all, he believed he would survive if he just kept walking. He did not want to die, because he also still hoped to see his parents again. So he didn't stop. He knew he must never stop walking and hoping.

The saddest thing that happened during this long walk was that many of the young boys lost their trust in finding any safety or help, and then they just sat down and gave up. "Oh, my feet hurt, and my blisters hurt so much, I cannot go another step. I cannot walk anymore." The other boys tried to encourage them to keep moving, but they refused. They sat at the side of the dirt path too exhausted and hopeless to go on.

After many days, Deng turned around and couldn't believe his eyes. It wasn't just Deng and a few other boys walking. Now there were thousands of boys walking along with them! There were over thirty thousand young boys walking in the hope of finding safety. Later they became known as "The Lost Boys of Sudan." Sadly, many of the boys died of starvation, injuries, and illness. The boys who were able to live through that difficult, month-long walk finally arrived in the country of Ethiopia.

The Lost Boys of Sudan Reach Ethiopia

In Ethiopia, the boys found safety in a refugee camp created for people who had no villages of their own. At last they were able to stop walking and enjoy some food and water. The food and water was provided by the UNHCR—United Nations High Commissioner for Refugees—and an organization called Save the Children, to help take care of the boys. Without that food and water, and the shelter of the camp, the boys would have died. The shelter became a home for them, a place of safety and community.

The boys stayed together in the camp for about four years. During that time a bond was formed among them. They were like family. Then, in 1991, when Deng was only ten years old, the camp was attacked by cruel armed rebels who had overthrown the government of Ethiopia. The boys were no longer safe in Ethiopia and were told to run in the direction of Sudan. The boys barely had time to race from the camp, and they were pursued by the attacking soldiers.

After two days of running, the boys came to the huge Gilo River on the border of Ethiopia and Sudan. In order to escape the soldiers, the boys had to cross the raging river, where some of them were attacked and killed by crocodiles. Others were killed by gunfire from the pursuing soldiers, and many of the boys drowned because they didn't know how to swim. Deng was able to survive because he grew up on the Nile River and knew how to swim.

The boys who survived the river crossing started walking into Sudan, finding safety at a refugee camp bordering Ethiopia called Pachalla Camp. Unfortunately, the safety in Pachalla lasted only six months because they were attacked by the Sudanese army once again. The army took many boys, especially the older ones, as prisoners. Deng was safe from being kidnapped because he was only ten years old.

Sudan

Gwalla

BOR
River Gilo

Panyindu

Pachalla

Ethiopia

Kakuma

Kenya

18

Walking Once Again

Once again the young boys were adrift. Far away from food and protection in the camp, they were very scared. They didn't know where to go or what would happen to them. They were no longer safe in Ethiopia or Sudan, so they began a journey toward the country of Kenya where they hoped to find safety. They began to do what they had done four years before. They started walking.

This time, the boys walked over one thousand miles. The long walk took them not just one month, or even six months, but more than twelve whole months—over one year—to get to northern Kenya.

Tragically, this very long and exhausting walk took many lives. The boys first had to cross the desert in the Sudan. Many of the boys died from illness, exhaustion, and starvation. It was hot and dry in the desert, and water and food were scarce. Although many boys died, many were saved because the United Nations dropped food from planes for them. Sometimes a truck would drive by and drop the food along their route. The boys had beans and corn, which they cooked over fires. They also got water at times from water trucks. By this time they had small utensils to cook with, and they had some clothes. The United Nations could not rescue the boys, but they did help many survive by providing food and water along their yearlong journey through the hot desert.

Sadly, some boys died not just from starvation or thirst but because they gave up hope. Those deaths were the saddest of all for Deng. When he saw

a young boy stop walking to sit under a tree, he knew that the boy had given up hope in his heart. Separating from the group meant that the boy would die within a day.

Whenever Deng felt that he just couldn't go one more step, he would remember the words of his parents: "Never give up hope, Deng." He would listen to his heart, but he would also listen to his growling stomach, and the hope of finding food would keep his thin, frail body moving onward. The group of boys he walked with was now like his family. They gave him strength, hope, and courage. Deng's greatest hope was that one day he might find his parents alive and be united with them. This hope kept him walking. And walking.

At Kakuma Refugee Camp in Kenya

When the group of boys finally reached Kenya in 1992, their numbers had gone from about thirty thousand down to about sixteen thousand. Deng was now about eleven years old. In Kenya they found safety at another refugee camp called Kakuma. There were almost one hundred thousand refugees at the camp, which was very, very crowded.

The food supply, which was provided by the United Nations and several countries, was not enough to feed all the people. To keep organized, the refugees were divided into smaller groups of about fifty. Then these groups divided among themselves into groups of about five or six boys. Each group received food for about fifteen days, which they cooked every evening and placed in two large bowls, from which they all ate together. They ate in the evening so they would not have to try to sleep on an empty stomach.

It was important for their survival that each group learn to share and work together. The group became like a family, and once again Deng learned the lesson of working together in community.

Even though Deng was always hungry because he was surviving on only one meal of beans and corn each day, he was happy because his group worked together well and supported each other. The United Nations had supplied them with clothes, and there were small wooden huts, which slept between four and five people. Deng felt safe, and he was glad that he didn't have to walk anymore or look for his next meal in the desert.

Deng Learns to Read

A very important part of Deng's life in the camp was school, which at first was just some benches under the trees. Later, buildings were made for a schoolhouse. Teachers came there to teach, and children were able to attend the school every day. Deng learned to read and write, and he learned about the outside world. His daily schooling gave him hope that there was something more in his future than just looking for food and shelter. He knew that education would provide him with an opportunity for a better life. School gave him a passion for learning that continues to this day, and inspired him to encourage other children to learn to read and write.

Still hoping to find his parents, Deng walked up and down and around the refugee camp. He looked and looked at all the people, but no matter how long he searched, he still didn't find the two people most important to him.

Deng spent nearly nine years in the refugee camp, where he made many friends. Still, at night he would dream the same dream over and over again.

He would dream of his own home, and the village he loved, and the songs they would sing and the celebrations they would have together. And he dreamed that one day he would be able to go back there and find his parents at last. This hope gave him a strong will to survive even in the toughest days when his belly wasn't full or when the dust and crowding in the camp seemed too much to bear. The hope in his heart, the hope his parents had given him, was his true friend—the friend that would never let him give up.

At one point Deng became quite ill from parasites. He was taken to a hospital in the refugee camp. His cousins in the camp, the ones from his village, took turns taking care of him, bringing him food, and sitting with him. They even slept there at night to watch over him. He was very weak and experienced terrible stomach pains and diarrhea, but he managed to survive.

Journey to a New Country

After many years, the United States heard about the poor conditions in the camp and offered to bring 3,800 boys to the United States for a chance at a better life. In 2001, after seven long interviews with people who asked him so many questions over and over again, Deng was one of the people selected to come to the United States to live in the city of San Jose, California. He was filled with many emotions. He was a bit scared, but also very excited. At the same time, he was filled with uncertainty and sadness. He had no idea what this new life would be like, and he was filled with a sense of anxiety and loss at leaving his friends. Some were like family to him, and the camp was like a village. But above all, he felt excitement and anticipation.

Deng knew that the United States offered him a chance for better education and a life outside of the refugee camps. To get to the United States, he had to take a very long plane ride. He was terrified! Imagine getting on an airplane for the very first time. After all those years of walking, now he was flying! Everything was unfamiliar and strange, from flying in the air above the clouds to being served food on trays and turning on the overhead lights in the cabin. Even the soft reclining seats were a new experience for Deng.

Deng Arrives in the United States

When Deng finally arrived in the United States, he found the country exciting but also strange and terrifying. First, there were the huge crowds at the airport, the tall buildings, and the big highways. Deng had never seen such sights, and he had difficulty understanding everything that he was seeing. Remember that he came from a very small village with no electricity or running water.

In his first few weeks, he experienced many, many things for the first time, such as grocery stores, toilets, light bulbs, telephones, and even clocks. While there were many kind Americans who helped introduce Deng and the other Lost Boys of Sudan to the new surroundings, staying connected to his friends from Southern Sudan who arrived with him was very important. They were a link between his past and his future. Their presence gave him a sense of belonging and security. Once again, Deng saw the importance of being together in community and being with people familiar with his culture.

Deng's determination to receive an education helped him overcome his fears and challenges. He worked very hard to learn better English at a community college. After community college he was proud to be accepted into San Jose State University in San Jose, California. Deng met many new people at school, but he still kept in touch with the other refugees from Southern Sudan who were also living in nearby parts of San Jose.

Deng often worked nights to support himself while he was going to school. His first job in the United States was as a stock clerk in a store. Even that was difficult, as he often didn't understand what people were asking him to find in the store. For example, he was asked to get a customer a blue gingham pad for a baby crib, but he didn't know what gingham was or even what a crib was. He had to work extra hard to learn new things, but his determination carried him through.

Deng Returns to His Village

In 2005, the long civil war between Northern and Southern Sudan finally ended, and a peace treaty was signed. Deng's heart warmed with excitement and joy when he heard that it was now safe to go back to the villages in Southern Sudan. He still had hope that his parents were alive, so when he had saved enough money from his job, he made the long journey back to Southern Sudan during his summer break from school. First there was a long trip by airplane from San Jose to Uganda, next a bus ride to Kakuma Camp and Lukichoggio in Kenya, then a bumpy trip by cargo plane to Bor Town, and finally after nine hours of walking on a dirt path, Deng arrived in his village. It had been so many years since he had been home, but fortunately, because he remembered the name of his village—Gwalla—he was able to locate it.

When he finally walked into his village, everyone wondered who he was, because when most of them had last seen him he was a very little boy. But he would go up to each one and kept repeating his name over and over again and asking the same question, "Are my parents in this village?" And then one person answered him with the words that made him nearly fall to the ground with shock. "Yes," the woman answered, "your mother arrived in this village just about two months ago, and your father arrived only days ago." Deng couldn't believe the good news. But he learned also that this very day was the day of his grandmother's funeral.

Running towards where the woman pointed, he was shocked that he recognized his mother, even though he hadn't seen her since he was just five years old. It had been nearly twenty years since they had last seen each other. At first, Deng's mother didn't recognize the big man in front of her as her son. She said to Deng, "I will know you are my son if you can tell me the special nickname I called you when you were little." There was complete silence as the villagers held their breath, wondering if Deng would remember a special name from so long ago.

Deng said, "Momma, you called me Makuol, which means little pumpkin!" Deng's mother screamed with joy and hugged him. The whole village let out shouts of joy and excitement. Where there had been a sorrowful feeling just moments before, there was now joy and celebration. Deng's father began to run around, shouting with joy.

Deng was finally home! He then realized that while it was very special that he had found his parents alive, his memories of home and family, the memories that he had carried in his heart all these years, could never be taken away. Home was in his heart, where it had always been.

Deng Raises Money to Help His Village

Deng was pleased to see his family, but he was sad that his village was in poor condition from the war and years of neglect. There were no paved roads or clean water in the well. There were no buildings for school. The women spent most of the day grinding corn by hand. Deng was determined to help. He vowed that the next time he returned to the village he would help to improve it in some way. He was filled with hope, and he knew what to do.

Deng went back to San Jose to finish school, graduating with a degree in health science. While he was going to school, he found time to give lectures at local schools and churches about his experiences and the conditions in Southern Sudan. His was a message of hope and courage. He stressed the importance of never giving up no matter what terrible things happened to you or what was in the way to try to stop your walk along the path. Deng said, "You must always stay connected to others in your community and keep yourself educated so you can not only help yourself but help others as well."

People were inspired that someone who had suffered for so long could use his life to help make a positive difference. Many people donated money so that Deng could help his village. The next summer, Deng returned to his village in Sudan with the money he collected. Deng installed a big machine to grind grain. This saved the young girls in the village many hours of grinding grain by hand, and so they had time to go to school. Another year, Deng had enough money to purchase materials to build a schoolhouse that sheltered three hundred students. The villagers donated the land for the school, helped dig the foundation, and made bricks for the walls. The children were proud to attend the school they helped build. The villagers were very happy and very proud of Deng.

It was a long, tough journey for Deng as a "Lost Boy of Sudan," but because he carried hope in his heart he never gave up. He never gave up, even when there were many times he could have stopped, separated from his group and sat under a tree to die, giving up his fight to live. But he never did that. Despite all that he went through, all the years of suffering, Deng made a positive difference for many people, especially those in Southern Sudan. He might be called a "Lost Boy of Sudan," but he is now a man who has found a purpose to believe in, and his hope is saving hundreds and hundreds of people today.

33

WORDS TO KNOW

1. **Animist (also called Animism)** —The belief that spirits live in all the things in nature. In Animism there can be spirits in animals, rocks, trees, rivers, thunder, mountains, etc.

<u>Sample sentence:</u>

Because I am an Animist, I get a lot of pleasure from talking to the tree spirits and the water spirits.

2. **Uncomplicated**—complicated means not simple or easy. *Un*complicated means simple or easy.

<u>Sample sentence:</u>

The directions were uncomplicated, so I was able to follow them with no trouble.

3. **Conflict**—struggle or battle. When there is a war, there is great conflict. Sometimes you can have a conflict with yourself when you are not sure what is the right thing to do. So you can have a conflict with someone else, or with yourself.

<u>Sample Sentence:</u>

There was a terrible conflict between two different parts of the country, which created a civil war.

4. **Resources** - the materials or supplies that a country or a person has to help them to live and grow. A country's resources could be things like rich soil for growing crops, forests for wood, or minerals like oil, copper or gold. A person's resources could be his intelligence, his good humor, or his ability to communicate.

The tiny country had no natural resources, so it had to depend on other countries for help.

5. **Urge**—a strong feeling or desire. When something happens that makes you feel you just *have* to do something, that feeling is an urge. The urge to survive, to live even though it is hard, is such a feeling.

Sample Sentence:

I was so happy when I saw that my lost brother was found that I had a great urge to hug him.

6. **Trudge**—to walk heavily, walk with heavy steps.

Sample Sentence:

We were so tired at the end of the day that we trudged home and went to bed.

7. **Borders**—The line between two countries is called a border, or a boundary. When a country *borders* another, it means that it is right next to it, and they share a boundary.

Sample Sentence:

The United States borders Canada to the north.

8. **Refugee**—a person who has been forced to leave his or her country because of war or other bad conditions, like an earthquake or other natural disaster.

Sample Sentence:

All the boys of Sudan who went to Ethiopia were refugees from Sudan.

9. **Adrift**—moving without control, or without direction.

Sample Sentence:

When the Lost Boys had to run away again, they didn't know where to go. They were adrift in the desert, like a boat floating on the ocean with no direction.

10. **Tragically**—very sadly. When something is tragic, it is very sad. If a very young child dies, we say it is a tragedy, or tragically, he died without getting to live his full life.

Sample Sentence:

Tragically, she could not get into the burning house to save the cat.

11. **Exhaustion**—being totally without any energy. If exhaustion continues for a long time, a person can become ill or die.

Sample Sentence:

We were overcome with exhaustion after the long hike up the mountain, and we finally got to rest.

12. **Frail**—very weak.

Sample Sentence:

After her long illness, she was very frail.

13. **United**—brought together or held together.

Sample Sentence:

The family was united again after many years of being apart.

14. **Reclining**—leaning back.

Sample Sentence:

The boy almost fell backwards when he leaned too hard in the reclining chair.

15. **Link**—connection, something that connects something to something else.

Sample Sentence:

My sister was a link between my brother and me, because she talked to both of us, but we didn't talk to each other very much.

16. **Retrieve**—to get, or get back. When you retrieve something, you get it and bring it to someone.

Sample Sentence:

I threw a stick in the water, and my dog ran to retrieve it.

17. **Gingham**—lightweight, plain woven cotton cloth, often with a design called checks, or little boxes.

Sample Sentence:

The baby's crib had gingham sheets and a gingham blanket.

18. **Determination**—a feeling of decision, of having a purpose you will not give up.

Sample Sentence:

His determination helped him to make it through all his difficulties.

19. **Treaty**—an agreement, usually made between two countries after a war or conflict.

Sample Sentence:

The United States and Japan signed a treaty after World War II.

20. **Neglect**—a condition that happens when something or someone is not taken care of. If a house is not taken care of it can be ruined by neglect. If you neglect your studies, you will fail in school.

Sample Sentence:

The house was in terrible condition because of neglect—no one had cleaned it or taken care of it for years.

21. **Vow**—promise

Sample Sentence:

I vowed that I would go to the gym every day for a month.

QUESTIONS TO THINK ABOUT

1. During his journey Deng had almost nothing. If you had to make such a journey, what do you think you would miss the most?

2. The war between the northern and southern parts of Sudan began because the North wanted things in the South, and they didn't want to share them. Because of this the whole country lost many lives, and still did not resolve the problem. What do you think might be a solution to this? How does this problem relate to your life? Do you ever get into fights that could be solved peaceably? How could you find another way to solve the problem without fighting?

3. What do you think was the hardest thing for the young men to get used to when they came to the United States? What would be most difficult for you if you had to go to live in another country?

4. What qualities did Deng have that helped him in his journey? What qualities do you have that might help you if you had to make such a journey? Are there any qualities you don't have but wish you had?

About Deng Ajak Jongkuch:

Deng Jongkuch was born in Southern Sudan in the rural village of Gwalla. In 1987, when he was only five years old, he was separated from his family while his village came under attack by government soldiers. He ran from his village, joining over 30,000 other "Lost Boys of Sudan." He survived long, grueling walks to seek food and shelter in refugee camps, first in Ethiopia and then in Kenya. In 2001, after spending many years in the Kakuma refugee camp in Kenya, Deng was selected along with 3,800 other Lost Boys to go to the United States. Deng worked hard to support himself and receive an education, graduating from California State University in San Jose in 2008 and completing a masters degree in public health from Touro University. Deng went back to his village in the summer of 2005 when the civil war ended and was joyfully reunited with his mother and father after 18 years. He was dismayed to find his village in very poor condition. There were no roads, clean water or schools. He became passionately committed to raising awareness and helping rebuild his and other villages in Southern Sudan. Deng helped start the nonprofit corporation Impact a Village; he gives frequent lectures to schools and churches in the San Francisco and Sacramento areas. Deng received his United States citizenship in 2010. He is married to a Sudanese woman and has three children.

About Lisa Frankel Wade:

Lisa Wade is president of the board of Impact a Village, Inc., and works closely with Deng Jongkuch to help build awareness and raise funds to improve education in Southern Sudan. She became interested in the plight of Southern Sudan after watching the documentary about the Lost Boys of Sudan called *God Grew Tired of Us*. For over 25 years Lisa has been the vice president of sales and marketing at Galil Motion Control, a high-tech company.

About the Lost Boys of Sudan:

The Lost Boys of Sudan refers to the nearly 30,000 boys who were displaced during the Sudanese Civil War that began in 1983 (over two million were killed). It was mostly boys who were displaced, as many were able to escape to the bush when their villages were attacked. The girls were carried off, and many of them were never seen again. The young boys made long, dangerous treks to find safety at relief camps in Kenya and Ethiopia. In 2001, about 3,800 Lost Boys were selected for resettlement in the United States.

About Impact a Village, Inc:

The mission of Impact a Village, Inc., is to improve education in villages throughout the world. The current focus is on villages in Southern Sudan, which has one of the lowest literacy rates in the world. Projects include building schools, providing school supplies, and hiring teachers. In the summer of 2009, Impact a Village provided funds to direct the building of a schoolhouse in the village of Malek, Southern Sudan. The primary school seats 300 children. Impact a Village, Inc., is a 501 (c)(3) nonprofit corporation. For more information or to make a donation, see www.ImpactAVillage.org

Children of Malek in School Uniforms

Villagers Digging Foundation for Malek School

Lisa Frankel Wade wrote Deng's story following his narration. Generous editing was provided by Davina Rubin and Cara Wilson-Granat. Illustrations were completed by Tereese Smaldino Radenbaugh. Many thanks for assistance by Cara France and Charisse Desmarais who are board members of Impact A Village.

Made in the USA
San Bernardino, CA
08 March 2017